TERMINAL BOUNDARIES

LAWRENCE WEINER
1969

PRIMARY INFORMATION
232 THIRD STREET, #A113
BROOKLYN, NY 11215

ISBN: 979-8-9910367-6-4

Terminal Boundaries

Terminal Boundaries

Lawrence Weiner

1969

~~Terminal Boundaries General~~

~~Terminal Boundaries General~~

~~Terminal Boundaries Specific~~

~~Terminal Boundaries Specific~~

An intrusion into an eastward flowing stre
am
An intrusion into a westward flowing strea
m
On or near the Continental Divide U.S.A.

Five gallons of red vegetable coloring pou
red into an eastward flowing stream on or
near the Continental Divide U.S.A.

Five gallons of red vegetable coloring pou
red into a westward flowing stream on or n
ear the Continental Divide U.S.A.

The joining of France Germany and Switzerl
and by rope

An equilateral rope triangle having Basel
Switzerland Germany and France as points

An amount of viscous non water soluble liq
uid poured into the Gulf Stream

One quart heavy grade motor oil poured int
o the Gulf Stream

One thousand dollars worth medium bulk mat
erial transfered from one country to anoth
er

1000 German Marks worth medium bulk material
transfered from one country to another

One regular rectangular object placed acro
ss an international boundary allowed to re
st then turned to and turned upon to intru
de the portion of one country into the oth
er

One regular rectangular object placed acro
ss the Mexican American boundary allowed t
o rest then turned to and turned upon to i
ntrude the portion of one country into the
other

Two fields in adjoining countries cratered
by simultaneous explosions

One field cratered by a structured explosi
on in or around Dublin Ireland
One field cratered by a structured explosi
on in or around Belfast North Ireland
Both fields cratered simultaneously

A stake set in the ground in direct line with a stake set in the ground of an adjacent country

A stake set in the ground fifty feet from
the Swiss German Border in Switzerland
A stake set in the ground fifty feet from
the German Swiss Border Germany
One stake in direct line with the other

An amount of material placed upon the ocea
n north of the Coaxial Cable
An amount of material placed upon the ocea
n south of the Coaxial Cable

50 pounds of lead placed upon the ocean no
rth of the Coaxial Cable
50 pounds of lead placed upon the ocean so
uth of the Coaxial Cable

Anti freeze in standard quantity poured up
on two opposing sides of the Antarctic Con
tinent and allowed to remain

One quart anti freeze poured upon the ice
Little America Ross Dependency Antarctica
and allowed to remain
One quart anti freeze poured upon the ice
Norway Station Princess Martha Coast Queen
Maud Land Antarctica and allowed to remain

A piece of ore broken placed one half appr
oximately upon the American side one half
approximately upon the Canadian side of th
e Saint Lawrence Seaway

A lodestone broken placed one half approxi
mately upon the American side one half app
roximately upon the Canadian side of the S
aint Lawrence Seaway

A concise explosion at the boundary common
to three countries

AACHEN GERMANY

A concise explosion near ~~Vaals Netherlands~~
upon the common boundary Germany Belgium a
nd the Netherlands

A ~~standard~~ rectangular object placed upon
a~~n~~ ~~international~~ boundary and allowed to r
est

One steel I beam placed upon a~~n internatio~~
~~nal~~ boundary and allowed to rest

A stone wall breached

A rural stone wall breached by detonated h
igh explosives

A river spanned by a temporary fixed ponto
n bridge

The River Clyde bridged by a temporary fix
ed floating bridge

An object tossed from one country to anoth
er

10 pounds Mercury tossed from Finland to S
weden

A flare ignited upon a boundary

The residue of a flare ignited upon a boun
dary

A non sinkable manufactured object thrown
into the American Falls Niagra Falls
A non sinkable manufactured object thrown
into the Canadian Falls Niagra Falls

A rubber ball thrown into the American Fal
ls Niagra Falls
A rubber ball thrown into the Canadian Fal
ls Niagra Falls

The shoulder of a highway continuous throu
gh two states set with signal flags

Signal flags set in the shoulder of a high
way continuous through Kansas City Kansas
and Kansas City Missouri
One set in each state

A trench dug from the high water marking t
o the low water marking upon a beach

A shallow trench dug from high water mark
to low ~~water~~ TIDE mark upon a North Atlantic be
ach

An object secured upon a boundary

An object secured upon a threshold

A rubber ball thrown at the sea

A rubber ball thrown on the sea

Düsseldorf, Germany

A natural water course diverted reduced
or displaced

Düsseldorf, Germany

A natural water course diverted reduced
or displaced

Amsterdam, Holland

A natural water course diverted reduced
or displaced

Stockholm, Sweden

A natural water course diverted reduced
or displaced

Stockholm, Sweden

A natural water course diverted reduced
or displaced

Oslo, Norway

A natural water course diverted reduced
or displaced

Saltstrume, Norway

A natural water course diverted reduced or
or displaced

A natural water course diverted reduced
or displaced

Bodø, Norway

A natural water course diverted reduced
or displaced

Bodø, Norway

A natural water course diverted reduced
or displaced

Bergen, Norway

A natural water course diverted reduced
or displaced

Inuvik, North West Territory, Canada

A natural water course diverted reduced
or displaced

Inuvik, North West Territory, Canada

Inuvik, North West Territory, Canada

A natural water course diverted reduced
or displaced

Inuvik, North West Territory, Canada

Inuvik, North West Territory, Canada

A natural water course diverted reduced
or displaced

Inuvik, North West Territory, Canada

Inuvik, North West Territory, Canada

A natural water course diverted reduced
or displaced

Yellowknife, North West Territory, Canada

A natural water course diverted reduced
or displaced

Piermont New Hampshire USA

A natural water course diverted reduced
or displaced

Piermont New Hampshire USA

A natural water course diverted reduced
or displaced

Etna New Hampshire USA

A natural water course diverted reduced
or displaced

Etna New Hampshire USA

Etna New Hampshire USA

A natural water course diverted reduced
or displaced

Etna New Hampshire USA

A natural water course diverted reduced
or displaced

Putney Vermont USA

A natural water course diverted reduced
or displaced

Windham College, Putney Vermont USA

A natural water course diverted reduced
or displaced

A natural water course diverted reduced
or displaced

Putney Vermont, U.S.A.

A natural water course diverted reduced
or displaced

A NATURAL WATER COURSE DIVERTED REDUCED OR DISPLACED

LAWRENCE WEINER
1969

PRIMARY INFORMATION
232 THIRD STREET, #A113
BROOKLYN, NY 11215

ISBN: 979-8-9910367-6-4